NEP 2020- AT A GLANCE FOR EDUCATORS

TOWARDS EXCELLENCE

DR. DHEERAJ MEHROTRA

ISBN 978-1-63806-273-8

Contents

PREFACE

NEP 2020- At a Glance for Educators,is a step towards getting to understand the concept of NEP and its roll out expectations from the side of the stakeholders in particular.

The books is a narration about what and why with expectations on making learning a priority for all. The objectives and the implementation is shared as a reader's point of view and governs the aspect of making learning a delightful attribute for all.

Looking foward to a great learning ahead.

Cheers & Happy Going!

Dheeraj Mehrotra

www.authordheerajmehrotra.com
tqmhead@aol.com

I
NEP - Quality Initiatives

THIS NATIONAL EDUCATION POLICY
AIMS AT BUILDING A GLOBAL BEST
EDUCATION SYSTEM ROOTED
IN INDIAN ETHOS, AND ALIGNED WITH
THE PRINCIPLES ENUNCIATED ABOVE,
THEREBY TRANSFORMING INDIA
INTO A GLOBAL KNOWLEDGE
SUPERPOWER.
New Education Policy
2020

NEW EDUCATION POLICY WAS LAUNCHED ON WEDNESDAY,
JULY 29. EARLIER, IN THE AFTERNOON THE UNION
CABINET APPROVED THE POLICY THAT AIMS TO
OVERHAUL THE COUNTRY'S EDUCATION SYSTEM. UNION
MINISTERS FOR INFORMATION AND BROADCASTING
(I&B)PRAKASH JAVADEKAR AND HUMAN RESOURCE
DEVELOPMENT (HRD) AND RAMESH POKHRIYAL NISHANK,
MADE THE ANNOUNCEMENT ON THE NEP- 2020. EARLIER
ON MAY 1, PRIME MINISTER NARENDRA MODI HAD
REVIEWED THE NEP- 2020, FOR WHICH DRAFT WAS
PREPARED BY A PANEL OF EXPERTS LED BY FORMER
INDIAN SPACE RESEARCH ORGANISATION (ISRO) CHIEF K
KASTURIRANGAN.
New Education Policy
2020

The Launch!

EDUCATION SECTOR TO GET 6% OF GDP, EARLIER IT WAS 1.7%

RAJYA SABHA MP, SUBRAMANIAN SWAMY TWEETED, "I WELCOME THE NEW EDUCATION POLICY OF THE MODI GOVERNMENT. I HAD A DISCUSSION WITH THE MOHD EARLIER WHICH I HAD TWEETED. MY SUGGESTION WAS THE EDUCATION MUST GET 6% OF GDP NOT THE PRESENT 1.7%. THIS HAS BEEN ACCEPTED IN THE NEW POLICY. MY CONGRATS."

New Education Policy
2020

THE NEP 2020 AIMS AT MAKING "INDIA A GLOBAL KNOWLEDGE SUPERPOWER".THE NEW ACADEMIC SESSION WILL BEGIN IN SEPTEMBER-OCTOBER - THE DELAY IS DUE TO THE UNPRECEDENTED CORONAVIRUS DISEASE (COVID-19) OUTBREAK - AND THE GOVERNMENT AIMS TO INTRODUCE THE POLICY BEFORE THE NEW SESSION KICKS IN.

New Education Policy
2020

NEP 2020: SCHOOL COMPLEXES TO BE USED FOR ADULT EDUCATION COURSES AFTER SCHOOL HOURS

USE OF SCHOOLS/ SCHOOL COMPLEXES BEYOND SCHOOL HOURS AND PUBLIC LIBRARY SPACES FOR ADULT EDUCATION COURSES WHICH WILL BE ICT-EQUIPPED WHEN POSSIBLE AND FOR OTHER COMMUNITY ENGAGEMENT AND ENRICHMENT ACTIVITIES

New Education Policy
2020

NEP 2020: MORE FOCUS ON VOCATIONAL STUDIES IN SCHOOL- LEVEL
EVERY CHILD TO LEARN AT LEAST ONE VOCATION AND EXPOSED TO SEVERAL MORE.

New Education Policy
2020

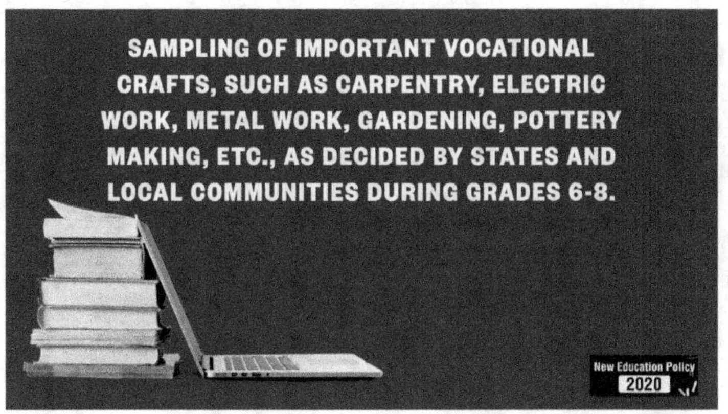
SAMPLING OF IMPORTANT VOCATIONAL
CRAFTS, SUCH AS CARPENTRY, ELECTRIC
WORK, METAL WORK, GARDENING, POTTERY
MAKING, ETC., AS DECIDED BY STATES AND
LOCAL COMMUNITIES DURING GRADES 6-8.
New Education Policy
2020

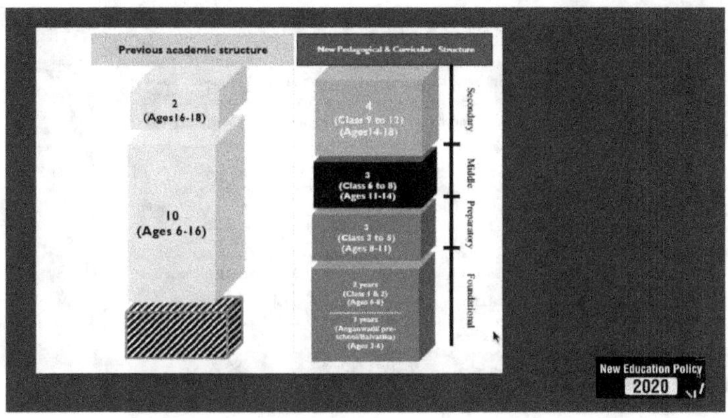
Previous academic structure
New Pedagogical & Curricular Structure
2
(Ages16-18)
10
(Ages 6-16)
4
(Class 9 to 12)
(Ages14-18)
3
(Class 6 to 8)
(Ages 11-14)
3
(Class 3 to 5)
(Ages 8-11)
2 years
(Class 1 & 2)
(Ages 6-8)
3 years
(Anganwadi/ pre-
school/Balvatika)
(Ages 3-6)
Secondary
Middle
Preparatory
Foundational
New Education Policy
2020

Breakdown of 5+3+3+4 structure

Foundational Stage (5): This stage of learning is suggested for children between 3 to 8 years. It involves a multi-level play activity-based learning in which a child will first spend 3 years at playschools and the kindergarten classes catering to ages 3 to 6. To this, classes 1 and 2 for students would also be added, with a focus on language development skills and play activity-based learning.

Preparatory Stage (3): This stage is for students between 8 to 11 years of age, learning in classes 3 to 5. The focus here shifts to play, discovery, activity-based and interactive classroom learning. The medium of instruction till Grade 5 would be the local language. Three languages will be taught to all students at this stage – and states can decide which ones.

Middle Stage (3): This stage will consist of students in classes 6 to 8. The focus here will shift to experiential learning in the sciences, mathematics, arts, social sciences and humanities.

Secondary Stage (4): Consisting of classes 9 to 12 students in this stage can choose any set of subjects from the available structure. The focus would be on greater critical thinking and flexibility.

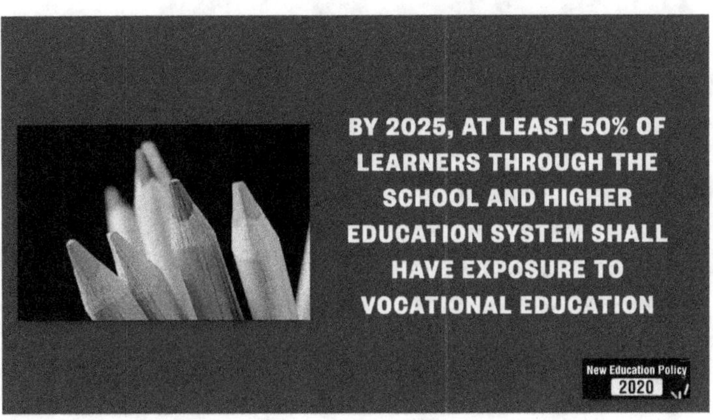
BY 2025, AT LEAST 50% OF LEARNERS THROUGH THE SCHOOL AND HIGHER EDUCATION SYSTEM SHALL HAVE EXPOSURE TO VOCATIONAL EDUCATION
New Education Policy
2020

A 10-DAY BAGLESS PERIOD SOMETIME DURING GRADES 6-8 TO INTERN WITH LOCAL VOCATIONAL EXPERTS SUCH AS CARPENTERS, GARDENERS, POTTERS, ARTISTS, ETC.
New Education Policy
2020

SIMILAR INTERNSHIP OPPORTUNITIES TO LEARN VOCATIONAL SUBJECTS TO STUDENTS THROUGHOUT GRADES 6-12, INCLUDING HOLIDAY PERIODS.
New Education Policy
2020

VOCATIONAL COURSES THROUGH ONLINE MODE WILL ALSO BE MADE AVAILABLE.
New Education Policy
2020

NEW EDUCATION POLICY 2020
1. 10+2 BOARD STRUCTURE IS DROPPED
2. NEW SCHOOL STRUCTURE WILL BE 5+3+3+4
3. UPTO 5 PRE SCHOOL, 6 TO 8 MID SCHOOL, 8
TO 11 HIGH SCHOOL , 12 ONWARDS GRADUATION
4. ANY DEGREE WILL BE 4 YEARS
5. 6TH STD ONWARDS VOCATIONAL COURSES
AVAILABLE
New Education Policy
2020

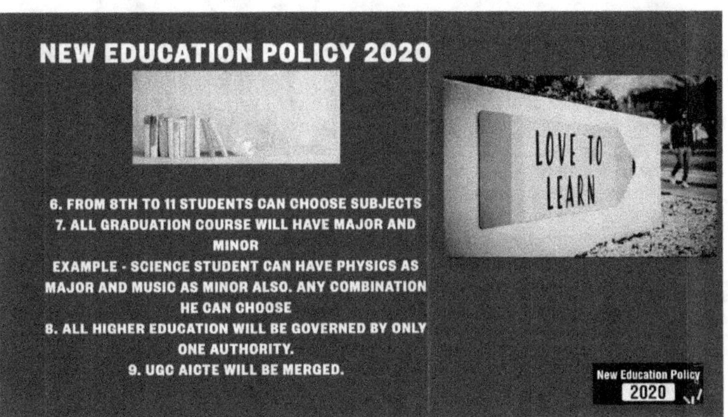
NEW EDUCATION POLICY 2020
LOVE TO LEARN
6. FROM 8TH TO 11 STUDENTS CAN CHOOSE SUBJECTS
7. ALL GRADUATION COURSE WILL HAVE MAJOR AND
MINOR
EXAMPLE - SCIENCE STUDENT CAN HAVE PHYSICS AS
MAJOR AND MUSIC AS MINOR ALSO. ANY COMBINATION
HE CAN CHOOSE
8. ALL HIGHER EDUCATION WILL BE GOVERNED BY ONLY
ONE AUTHORITY.
9. UGC AICTE WILL BE MERGED.
New Education Policy
2020

NEW EDUCATION POLICY 2020

10. ALL UNIVERSITY GOVERNMENT, PRIVATE, OPEN, DEEMED, VOCATIONAL ETC
WILL HAVE SAME GRADING AND OTHER RULES.
11. NEW TEACHER TRAINING BOARD WILL BE SETUP FOR ALL KINDS OF
TEACHERS IN COUNTRY, NO STATE CAN CHANGE
12. SAME LEVEL OF ACCREDITATION TO ANY COLLAGE , BASED ON ITS RATING
COLLAGE WILL GET AUTONOMOUS RIGHTS AND FUNDS.
13. NEW BASIC LEARNING PROGRAM WILL BE CREATED BY GOVERNMENT FOR
PARENTS TO TEACH CHILDREN UPTO 3 YEARS IN HOME AND FOR PRE SCHOOL 3
TO 6
14. MULTIPLE ENTRY AND EXIT FROM ANY COURSE
15. CREDIT SYSTEM FOR GRADUATION FOR EACH YEAR STUDENT WILL GET SOME
CREDITS WHICH HE CAN UTILIZE IF HE TAKES BREAK IN COURSE AND COME
BACK AGAIN TO COMPLETE COURSE

NEW EDUCATION POLICY 2020 IS ANNOUNCED

16. ALL SCHOOLS EXAMS WILL BE SEMESTER WISE TWICE A YEAR
17. THE SYLLABUS WILL BE REDUCED TO CORE KNOWLEDGE OF ANY SUBJECT ONLY
18. MORE FOCUS ON STUDENT PRACTICAL AND APPLICATION KNOWLEDGE
19. FOR ANY GRADUATION COURSE IF STUDENT COMPLETE ONLY ONE YEAR HE WILL GET A
BASIC CERTIFICATE, IF HE COMPLETE TWO YEARS THEN HE WILL GET DIPLOMA CERTIFICATE
AND IF HE COMPLETE FULL COURSE THEN HE WILL GET DEGREE CERTIFICATE. SO NO YEAR OF
ANY STUDENT WILL VE VESTED IF HE BREAK THE COURSE IN BETWEEN.
20.ALL THE GRADUATION COURSE FEED OF ALL UNIVERSITIES WILL BE GOVERN BY SINGLE
AUTHORITY WITH CAPPING ON EACH COURSE.

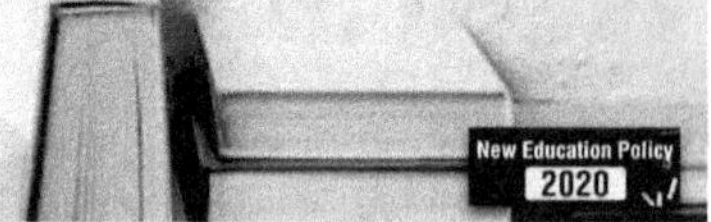

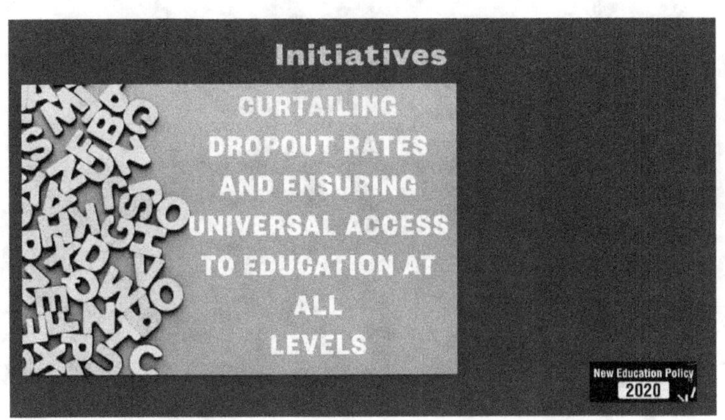
Initiatives
CURTAILING
DROPOUT RATES
AND ENSURING
UNIVERSAL ACCESS
TO EDUCATION AT
ALL
LEVELS
New Education Policy
2020

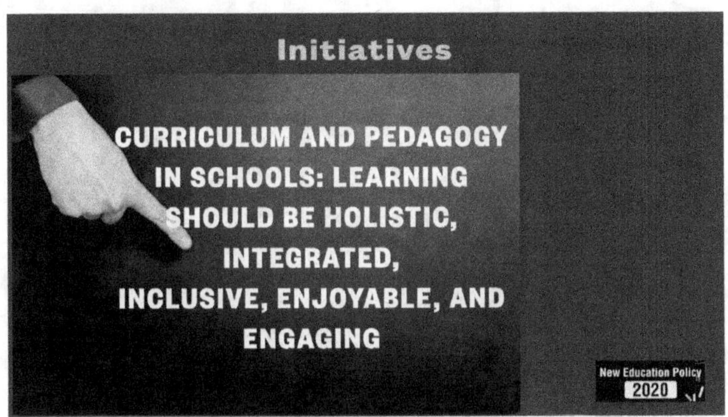
Initiatives
CURRICULUM AND PEDAGOGY
IN SCHOOLS: LEARNING
SHOULD BE HOLISTIC,
INTEGRATED,
INCLUSIVE, ENJOYABLE, AND
ENGAGING
New Education Policy
2020

Initiatives
CURRICULAR INTEGRATION OF ESSENTIAL SUBJECTS AND SKILLS
New Education Policy
2020

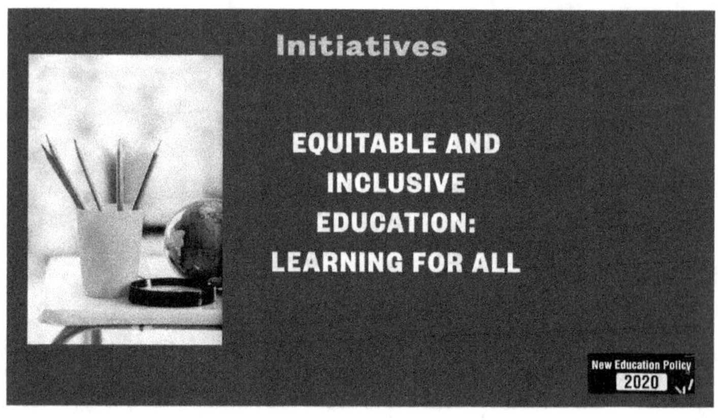
Initiatives
EQUITABLE AND INCLUSIVE EDUCATION: LEARNING FOR ALL
New Education Policy
2020

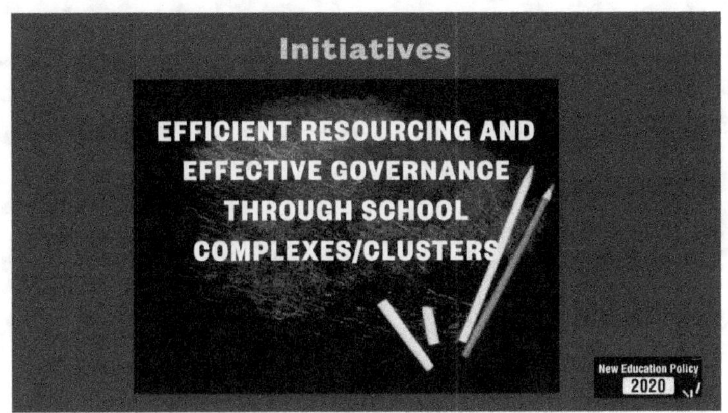
Initiatives
EFFICIENT RESOURCING AND
EFFECTIVE GOVERNANCE
THROUGH SCHOOL
COMPLEXES/CLUSTERS
New Education Policy
2020

Initiatives
STANDARD-
SETTING AND
ACCREDITATION
FOR SCHOOL
EDUCATION
New Education Policy
2020

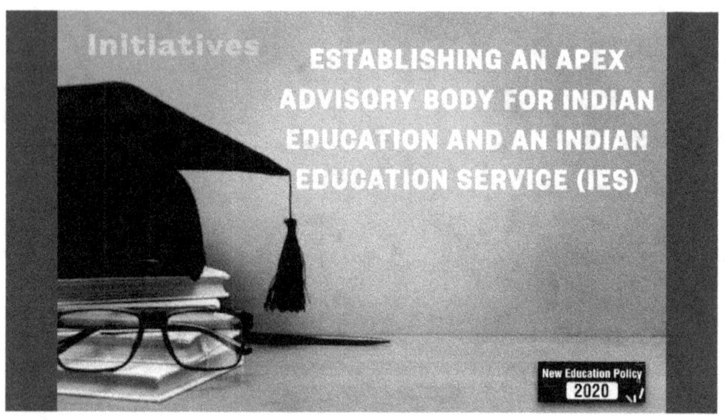
Initiatives
ESTABLISHING AN APEX
ADVISORY BODY FOR INDIAN
EDUCATION AND AN INDIAN
EDUCATION SERVICE (IES)
New Education Policy
2020

Initiatives
ESTABLISHING AN
APEX ADVISORY
BODY FOR INDIAN
EDUCATION AND
AN INDIAN
EDUCATION
SERVICE (IES)
New Education Policy
2020

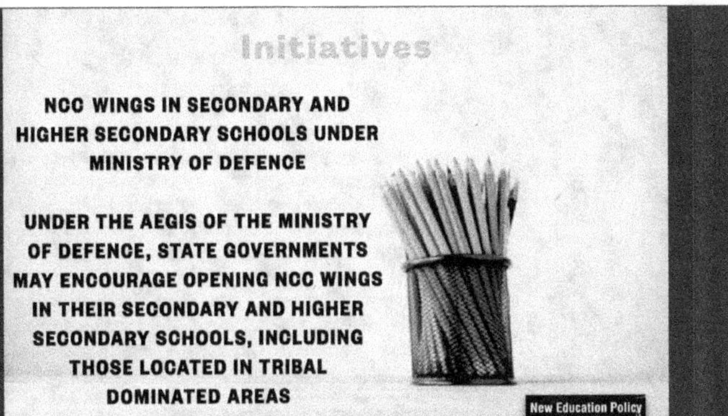
Initiatives
NCC WINGS IN SECONDARY AND
HIGHER SECONDARY SCHOOLS UNDER
MINISTRY OF DEFENCE

UNDER THE AEGIS OF THE MINISTRY
OF DEFENCE, STATE GOVERNMENTS
MAY ENCOURAGE OPENING NCC WINGS
IN THEIR SECONDARY AND HIGHER
SECONDARY SCHOOLS, INCLUDING
THOSE LOCATED IN TRIBAL
DOMINATED AREAS
New Education Policy
2020

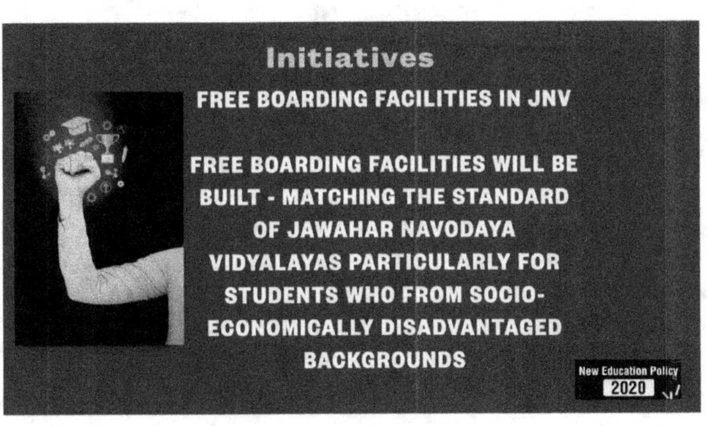
Initiatives
FREE BOARDING FACILITIES IN JNV

FREE BOARDING FACILITIES WILL BE
BUILT - MATCHING THE STANDARD
OF JAWAHAR NAVODAYA
VIDYALAYAS PARTICULARLY FOR
STUDENTS WHO FROM SOCIO-
ECONOMICALLY DISADVANTAGED
BACKGROUNDS
New Education Policy
2020

Initiatives

DEDICATED UNIT FOR DIGITAL AND ONLINE LEARNING.

A DEDICATED UNIT FOR THE PURPOSE OF ORCHESTRATING THE BUILDING OF DIGITAL INFRASTRUCTURE, DIGITAL CONTENT AND CAPACITY BUILDING WILL BE CREATED IN THE MHRD TO LOOK AFTER THE E-EDUCATION NEEDS OF BOTH SCHOOL AND HIGHER EDUCATION. A COMPREHENSIVE SET OF RECOMMENDATIONS FOR PROMOTING ONLINE EDUCATION CONSEQUENT TO THE RECENT RISE IN EPIDEMICS AND PANDEMICS IN ORDER TO ENSURE PREPAREDNESS WITH ALTERNATIVE MODES OF QUALITY EDUCATION WHENEVER AND WHEREVER TRADITIONAL AND IN-PERSON MODES OF EDUCATION ARE NOT POSSIBLE, HAS BEEN COVERED

Traits

Innovation/ Passion/ Creative Thinking on priority!

Holistic in nature!

It prepares for Creative/ Communicative/ empowered society.

Initiatives

NATIONAL SCHOLARSHIP PORTAL FOR SC, ST, OBC, SEDGS STUDENTS TO BE EXPANDED

EFFORTS WILL BE MADE TO INCENTIVIZE THE MERIT OF STUDENTS BELONGING TO SC, ST, OBC, AND OTHER SEDGS. THE NATIONAL SCHOLARSHIP PORTAL WILL BE EXPANDED TO SUPPORT, FOSTER, AND TRACK THE PROGRESS OF STUDENTS RECEIVING SCHOLARSHIPS. PRIVATE HEIS WILL BE ENCOURAGED TO OFFER LARGER NUMBERS OF FREE SHIPS AND SCHOLARSHIPS TO THEIR STUDENTS.

New Education Policy
2020

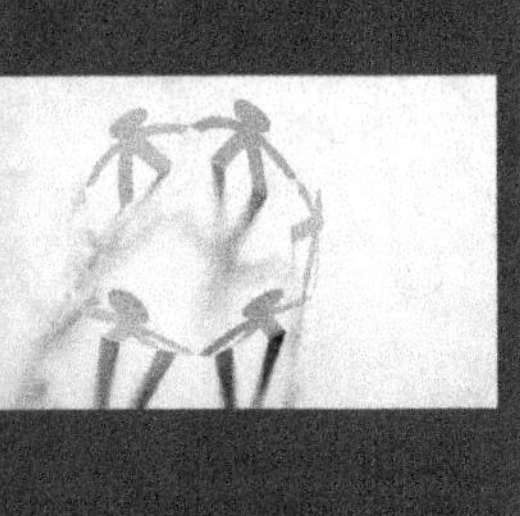

Initiatives

MINIMUM QUALIFICATION FOR TEACHING - 4 YEAR INTEGRATED B.ED DEGREE

A NEW AND COMPREHENSIVE NATIONAL CURRICULUM FRAMEWORK FOR TEACHER EDUCATION, NCFTE 2021, WILL BE FORMULATED BY THE NCTE IN CONSULTATION WITH NCERT. BY 2030, THE MINIMUM DEGREE QUALIFICATION FOR TEACHING WILL BE A 4-YEAR INTEGRATED B.ED. DEGREE .STRINGENT ACTION WILL BE TAKEN AGAINST SUBSTANDARD STAND-ALONE TEACHER EDUCATION INSTITUTIONS (TEIS).

New Education Policy
2020

Initiatives

THREE LANGUAGE LEARNED BY CHILDREN WILL BE THE CHOICE OF STATE, REGIONS AND STUDENTS

THE THREE-LANGUAGE LEARNED BY CHILDREN WILL BE THE CHOICES OF STATES, REGIONS, AND OF THE STUDENTS, SO LONG AS AT LEAST TWO OF THE THREE LANGUAGES ARE NATIVE TO INDIA.

Initiatives

MEDIUM OF INSTRUCTION WILL BE THE LOCAL/ REGIONAL LANGUAGE

WHEREVER POSSIBLE, THE MEDIUM OF INSTRUCTION UNTIL AT LEAST GRADE 5, BUT PREFERABLY TILL GRADE 8 AND BEYOND, WILL BE THE HOME LANGUAGE/ MOTHER TONGUE/LOCAL LANGUAGE/ REGIONAL LANGUAGE.

Initiatives

INDIAN SIGN LANGUAGE TO BE STANDARDISED ACROSS THE COUNTRY

INDIAN SIGN LANGUAGE (ISL) WILL BE STANDARDIZED ACROSS THE COUNTRY, AND NATIONAL AND STATE CURRICULUM MATERIALS DEVELOPED, FOR USE BY STUDENTS WITH HEARING IMPAIRMENT

Initiatives

NO HARD SEPARATION OF STREAMS FOR STUDENTS
STUDENTS WILL BE GIVEN INCREASED FLEXIBILITY AND CHOICE OF SUBJECTS TO STUDY, PARTICULARLY IN SECONDARY SCHOOL - INCLUDING SUBJECTS IN PHYSICAL EDUCATION, THE ARTS AND CRAFTS, AND VOCATIONAL SKILLS
THERE WILL BE NO HARD SEPARATION AMONG 'CURRICULAR', 'EXTRACURRICULAR', OR 'CO-CURRICULAR', AMONG 'ARTS', 'HUMANITIES', AND 'SCIENCES', OR BETWEEN 'VOCATIONAL' OR 'ACADEMIC' STREAMS. SUBJECTS SUCH AS PHYSICAL EDUCATION, THE ARTS AND CRAFTS, AND VOCATIONAL SKILLS, IN ADDITION TO SCIENCE, HUMANITIES, AND MATHEMATICS, WILL BE INCORPORATED THROUGHOUT THE SCHOOL CURRICULUM.

EACH OF THE FOUR STAGES OF SCHOOL EDUCATION, MAY CONSIDER MOVING TOWARDS A SEMESTER OR ANY OTHER SYSTEM THAT ALLOWS THE INCLUSION OF SHORTER MODULES

Initiatives

EXPERIENTIAL LEARNING IN ALL STAGES

EXPERIENTIAL LEARNING WILL INCLUDE HANDS-ON LEARNING, ARTS-INTEGRATED AND SPORTS-INTEGRATED EDUCATION, STORY-TELLING-BASED PEDAGOGY, AMONG OTHERS, AS STANDARD PEDAGOGY . CLASSROOM TRANSACTIONS WILL SHIFT, TOWARDS COMPETENCY-BASED LEARNING AND EDUCATION

www.authordheerajmehrotra.com

Initiatives

CONTENT WILL FOCUS ON IDEA, APPLICATION, PROBLEM- SOLVING

THE MANDATED CONTENT WILL FOCUS ON KEY CONCEPTS, IDEAS, APPLICATIONS, AND PROBLEM- SOLVING. TEACHING AND LEARNING WILL BE CONDUCTED IN A MORE INTERACTIVE MANNER

Initiatives

CURRICULUM CONTENT TO BE REDUCED

CURRICULUM CONTENT WILL BE REDUCED IN EACH SUBJECT TO ITS CORE ESSENTIALS, AND MAKE SPACE FOR CRITICAL THINKING AND MORE HOLISTIC, INQUIRY-BASED, DISCOVERY-BASED, DISCUSSION-BASED, AND ANALYSIS-BASED LEARNING.

Initiatives

NUTRITION AND HEALTH CARDS, REGULAR HEALTH CHECK-UPS FOR SCHOOL STUDENTS

THE NUTRITION AND HEALTH (INCLUDING MENTAL HEALTH) OF CHILDREN WILL BE ADDRESSED, THROUGH HEALTHY MEALS AND REGULAR HEALTH CHECK-UPS, AND HEALTH CARDS WILL BE ISSUED TO MONITOR THE SAME.

Initiatives

360 DEGREE HOLISTIC REPORT CARD FOR STUDENTS

STUDENTS WILL GET 360 DEGREE HOLISTIC REPORT CARD, WHICH WILL NOT ONLY INFORM ABOUT THE MARKS OBTAINED BY THEM IN SUBJECTS, BUT ALSO THEIR SKILLS AND OTHER IMPORTANT POINTS.

Initiatives

CODING TO BE TAUGHT FROM CLASS 6 ONWARDS

STUDENTS OF CLASS 6 AND ONWARDS WILL BE TAUGHT CODING IN SCHOOLS AS A PART OF 21ST CENTURY SKILLS, SCHOOL EDUCATION SECRETARY SAID.

New Education Policy
2020
CONCLUSION
#NEP: 2020 (School Education)

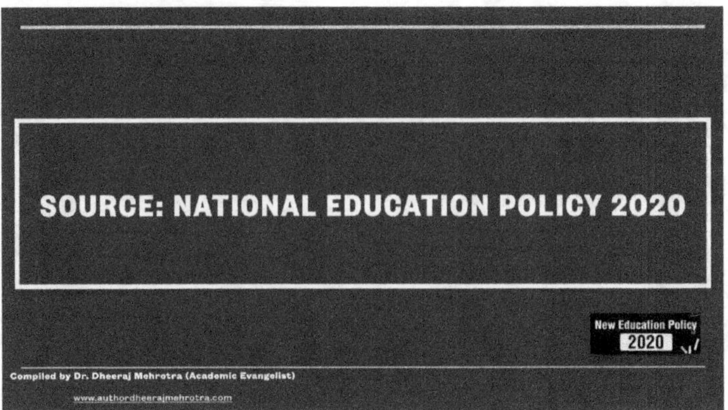
SOURCE: NATIONAL EDUCATION POLICY 2020
New Education Policy
2020
Compiled by Dr. Dheeraj Mehrotra (Academic Evangelist)
www.authordheerajmehrotra.com

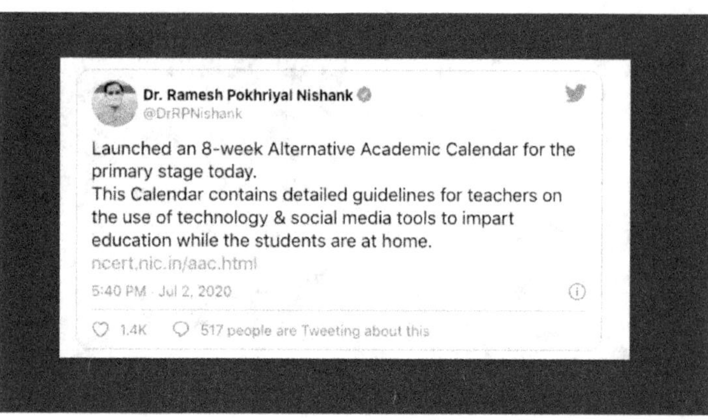

Subject-Wise Study Plan

According to an official release, the alternative calendar has been designed with an aim to "engage students meaningfully during their stay at home due to COVID-19."

The calendar contains an eight-week study plan for different subjects of the primary classes, along with activities, resources, and links to different e-content prepared by the HRD ministry.

"The calendar contains week-wise plan consisting of interesting and challenging activities, with reference to theme or chapter taken from syllabus or textbook. Most importantly, it maps the themes with the learning outcomes," an official statement said.

"The purpose of mapping of themes with learning outcomes is to facilitate teachers or parents to assess the progress in the learning of children and also to go beyond textbooks. The activities given in the calendar focus on learning outcomes and can thus be achieved through any resource including the textbooks...." the statement added.

Detailed activities for Mathematics, Geography, Hindi, and Urdu for Classes 1 and 2; and Mathematics, Geography, Hindi, Urdu, and Environmental Studies for Classes 3 to 5 along with Art Education and Health and Physical Education has been included in the calendar.

Alternative Academic Calendar

In this period of Covid-19, which is declared as a global pandemic, our teachers, parents, and students have to remain at homes to prevent its spread in the community. In this situation, it is our responsibility to provide them with multiple alternative ways of learning at home through interesting activities. It is necessary because in the present environment of stress we have to not only keep our children busy but also to maintain continuity of their learning in their new classes. In this context, NCERT has developed an Alternative Academic Calendar for all the stages of school education.

- Eight Week Alternative Academic Calendar for the Upper Primary Stage Part II- English || Hindi
- Eight Week Alternative Academic Calendar for the Primary Stage Part I- English || Hindi
- Alternative Academic Calendar for Students Primary-English
- Alternative Academic Calendar for Students Primary-Hindi
- Alternative Academic Calendar for Students Upper Primary-English
- Alternative Academic Calendar for Students Upper Primary-Hindi
- Alternative Academic Calendar for Students Secondary-English
- Alternative Academic Calendar for Students Secondary-Hindi
- Alternative Academic Calendar for Students Higher Secondary-English
- Alternative Academic Calendar for Students Higher Secondary-Hindi
- Cyber Safety and Security: Online Learning in Times of COVID-19- English || Hindi

https://ncert.nic.in/alternative-academic-calendar.php

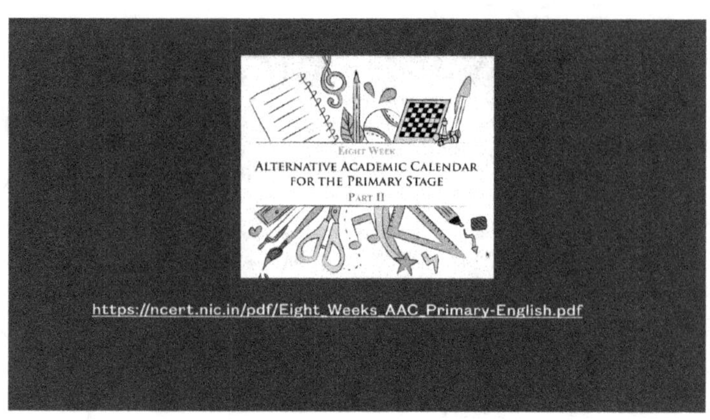
EIGHT WEEK
ALTERNATIVE ACADEMIC CALENDAR
FOR THE PRIMARY STAGE
PART II
https://ncert.nic.in/pdf/Eight_Weeks_AAC_Primary-English.pdf

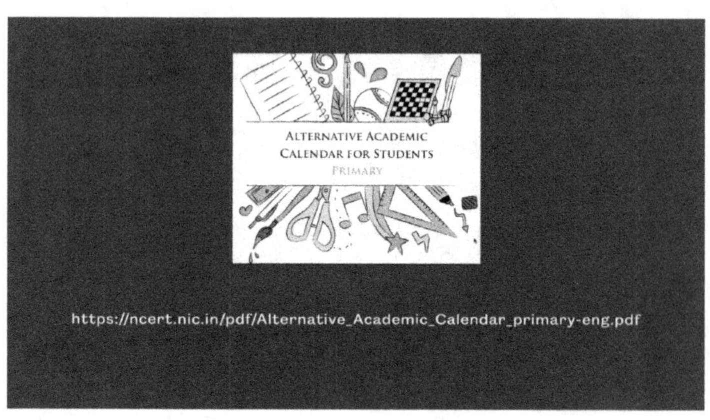
ALTERNATIVE ACADEMIC
CALENDAR FOR STUDENTS
PRIMARY
https://ncert.nic.in/pdf/Alternative_Academic_Calendar_primary-eng.pdf

II

ECCE Early Childhood Care Education

ECCE
Early Childhood Care Education
Children are the Priority!
Change is the Reality!
Collaboration is the Strategy!
An Initiative by www.facebook.com/rockstarteachers

An Initiative by www.facebook.com/rockstarteachers

Early childhood care and education (ECCE) is more than preparation for primary school. It aims at the holistic development of a child's social, emotional, cognitive and physical needs in order to build a solid and broad foundation for lifelong **learning** and wellbeing.

An Initiative by www.facebook.com/rockstarteachers

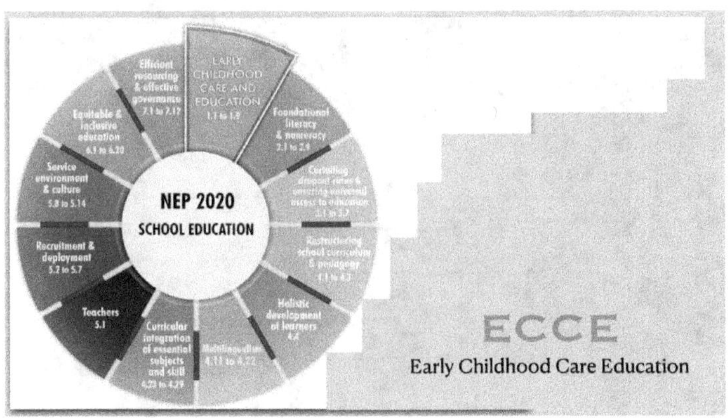

Early Childhood Care Education

ECCE should be included as an integral part of the RTE Act. 4. NCERT to develop integrated Curricular. intended **for** parents, Anganwadi workers and teachers with focus on health and nutrition of mother & child and cognitive and emotional stimulation of the child.

An Initiative by www.facebook.com/rockstarteachers

An Initiative by www.facebook.com/rockstarteachers

Pic: Courtesy Unesco.org

Pic: Courtesy Unesco.org

National Education Policy 2020

Currently, children in the age group of 3-6 are not covered in the 10+2 structure as Class 1 begins at age 6. In the new 5+3+3+4 structure, a strong base of Early Childhood Care and Education (ECCE) from age 3 is also included, which is aimed at promoting better overall learning, development, and well-being.

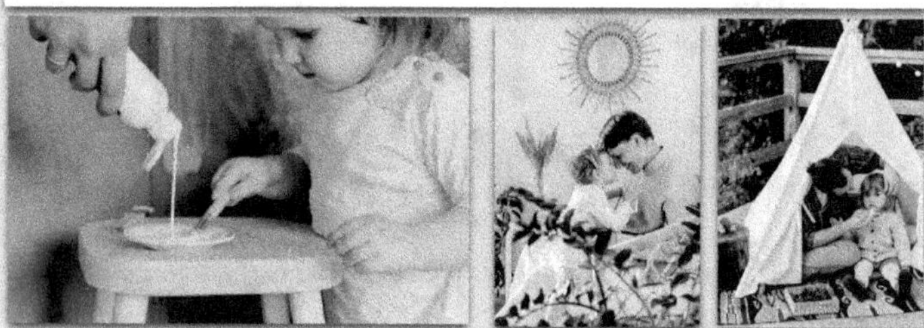

1. Early Childhood Care and Education: The Foundation of Learning

1.1. Over 85% of a child's cumulative brain development occurs prior to the age of 6, indicating the critical importance of appropriate care and stimulation of the brain in the early years in order to ensure healthy brain development and growth. Presently, quality ECCE is not available to crores of young children, particularly children from socio-economically disadvantaged backgrounds. Strong investment in ECCE has the potential to give all young children such access, enabling them to participate and flourish in the educational system throughout their lives. Universal provisioning of quality early childhood development, care, and education must thus be achieved as soon as possible, and no later than 2030, to ensure that all students entering Grade 1 are school ready.

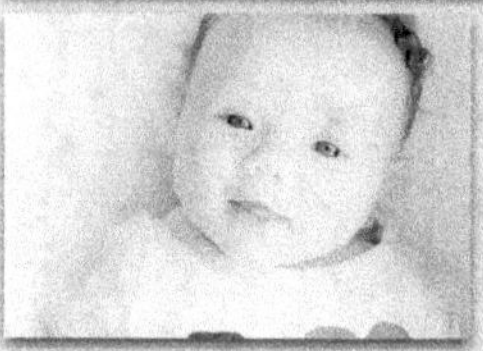

1. Early Childhood Care and Education: The Foundation of Learning

1.2. ECCE ideally consists of flexible, multi-faceted, multi-level, play-based, activity-based, and inquiry-based learning, comprising of alphabets, languages, numbers, counting, colours, shapes, indoor and outdoor play, puzzles and logical thinking, problem-solving, drawing, painting and other visual art, craft, drama and puppetry, music and movement. It also includes a focus on developing social capacities, sensitivity, good behaviour, courtesy, ethics, personal and public cleanliness, teamwork, and cooperation. The overall aim of ECCE will be to attain optimal outcomes in the domains of: physical and motor development, cognitive development, socio-emotional-ethical development, cultural/artistic development, and the development of communication and early language, literacy, and numeracy.

1. Early Childhood Care and Education: The Foundation of Learning

1.3. A National Curricular and Pedagogical Framework for Early Childhood Care and Education (NCPFECCE) for children up to the age of 8 will be developed by NCERT in two parts, namely, a sub-framework for 0-3 year-olds, and a sub-framework for 3-8 year-olds, aligned with the above guidelines, the latest research on ECCE, and national and international best practices. In particular, the numerous rich local traditions of India developed over millennia in ECCE involving art, stories, poetry, games, songs, and more, will also be suitably incorporated. The framework will serve as a guide both for parents and for early childhood care and education institutions.

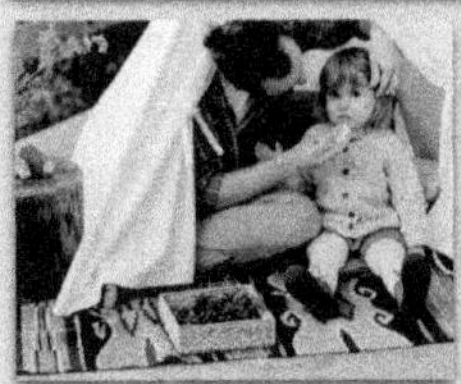

1. Early Childhood Care and Education: The Foundation of Learning

1.4. The overarching goal will be to ensure universal access to high-quality ECCE across the country in a phased manner. Special attention and priority will be given to districts and locations that are particularly socio-economically disadvantaged. ECCE shall be delivered through a significantly expanded and strengthened system of early-childhood education institutions consisting of (a) stand-alone Anganwadis; (b) Anganwadis co-located with primary schools; (c) pre-primary schools/sections covering at least age 5 to 6 years co-located with existing primary schools; and (d) stand-alone pre-schools - all of which would recruit workers/teachers specially trained in the curriculum and pedagogy of ECCE.

1. Early Childhood Care and Education: The Foundation of Learning

1.5. For universal access to ECCE, Anganwadi Centres will be strengthened with high-quality infrastructure, play equipment, and well-trained Anganwadi workers/teachers. Every Anganwadi will have a well-ventilated, well-designed, child-friendly and well-constructed building with an enriched learning environment. Children in Anganwadi Centres shall take activity-filled tours - and meet the teachers and students of their local primary schools, in order to make the transition from Anganwadi Centres to primary schools a smooth one. Anganwadis shall be fully integrated into school complexes/clusters, and Anganwadi children, parents, and teachers will be invited to attend and participate in school/school complex programmes and vice versa.

1. Early Childhood Care and Education: The Foundation of Learning

1.6. It is envisaged that prior to the age of 5 every child will move to a "Preparatory Class" or "Balavatika" (that is, before Class 1), which has an ECCE-qualified teacher. The learning in the Preparatory Class shall be based primarily on play-based learning with a focus on developing cognitive, affective, and psychomotor abilities and early literacy and numeracy. The mid-

day meal programme shall also be extended to the Preparatory Classes in primary schools. Health check-ups and growth monitoring that are available in the Anganwadi system shall also be made available to Preparatory Class students of Anganwadi as well as of primary schools.

1. Early Childhood Care and Education: The Foundation of Learning

1.7. To prepare an initial cadre of high-quality ECCE teachers in Anganwadis, current Anganwadi workers/teachers will be trained through a systematic effort in accordance with the curricular/pedagogical framework developed by NCERT. Anganwadi workers/teachers with qualifications of 10+2 and above shall be given a 6-month certificate programme in ECCE; and those with lower educational qualifications shall be given a one-year diploma programme covering early literacy, numeracy, and other relevant aspects of ECCE. These programmes may be run through digital/distance mode using DTH channels as well as smartphones, allowing teachers to acquire ECCE qualifications with minimal disruption to their current work. The ECCE training of Anganwadi workers/teachers will be mentored by the Cluster Resource Centres of the School Education Department which shall hold at least one monthly contact class for continuous assessment. In the longer term, State Governments shall prepare cadres of professionally qualified educators for early childhood care and education, through stage-specific professional training, mentoring mechanisms, and career mapping. Necessary facilities will also be created for the initial professional preparation of these educators and their Continuous Professional Development (CPD).

1. Early Childhood Care and Education: The Foundation of Learning

1.8. ECCE will also be introduced in Ashramshalas in tribal-dominated areas and in all formats of alternative schooling in a phased manner. The process for integration and implementation of ECCE in Ashramshalas and alternative schooling will be similar to that detailed above.

An Initiative by www.facebook.com/rockstarteachers

1. Early Childhood Care and Education: The Foundation of Learning

1.9. The responsibility for ECCE curriculum and pedagogy will lie with MHRD to ensure its continuity from pre-primary school through primary school, and to ensure due attention to the foundational aspects of education. The planning and implementation of early childhood care and education curriculum will be carried out jointly by the Ministries of HRD, Women and Child Development (WCD), Health and Family Welfare (HFW), and Tribal Affairs. A special joint task force will be constituted for continuous guidance of the smooth integration of early childhood care and education into school education.

An Initiative by www.facebook.com/rockstarteachers

Thank You!
SOURCE:
National Education Policy
An Initiative by www.facebook.com/rockstarteachers
https://www.mhrd.gov.in/sites/upload_files/mhrd/files/NEP_Final_English_o.pdf

III

Quality Education as a Priority

Teach me something new Maa'm. This is already in the book!! Comes the sound reply from the kids in a normal classroom.

Nurturing young minds via expertise of digital tools has had its inception with pride in nearly all fragments of learning today. The cyber based revolution of the learning community has had a dwelling effect on its dwellings and the new age digital learners want speed and where – ever content and assessment of their tasks. This abstract defines and declares an empirical reach on new age demands and necessities to make the learning more clear, obvious and desirable in the distracted world of today where the children are digitalized themselves of their dependence on technology and self-oriented learning. To the surprise of many, few years from now, the very iconic symbols of academic delivery, the hard bound books, chalk, duster and above all the desks and tables, may soon become mere a historical representation of the way the teaching was delivered at schools. The tech culture has revolutionised the very means of living and learning and is expected to pound over leaps in time to come bringing more of liberty, individuality and choice of learning to the masses. **Technology is now an essential part of our daily world and educators are creatively using it in the classroom and beyond.** Thanks to the power and governance of the Cloud Computing that we tend to deliver a one stop solution for schools to install and make a role towards Quality integrated with Excellence within the school and its wider spectrum of boundaries in a big way.

Managing the Googlers and TECH generation

There is an urgent need for defines and drafts as an essentiality for schools to ponder over the requirement of a cloud presence of their delivery via involvement of all stake holders. The objective has to make all the stake holders viz. the students, teachers, parents and the society as a whole, empowered, connected, engaged and successful. What is desired as of now is the combination of a Knowledge Hub Resource proposed by schools with an essence of Knowledge Transfer, Knowledge Sharing and Knowledge Community. The desire and demand for this Knowledge Hub is shared towards feedback and is a proposal to uplift the proposition towards Quality Learning Platform using the three sub ways viz.

• Knowledge Transfer• Knowledge Sharing• Knowledge Community

How do we understand where education systems and schools are?

Relating to aspect of this study, it is fertile to note that the data analysis relates to the continuous LIKES on their social networking platform but in reality and of demand. The scenario has to be fed in real life schooling environments and need to be made public among the intenders of knowledge delivery and sharing under the pretext of making the Learning Happen in classrooms and beyond. The objective has to be to *Cure Ignorance* via collaborations of teacher led incentives and uploads, there appears a sound preface that we conclude what is a desire and what is a demand by the schools today.

A general feedback by teachers and practitioners in the field of education needs to be analysed. To explore improvement via innovation is a definition to the new framework today. This helps the knowledge vendors to understand the education system and its change being desired at a common pace.

The objective to implement technology of a complete Knowledge Hub, integrated with sharing, transfer and collaborate, has to have an ultimate provision to deliver the greatest impact on learning, including school management and the best ever classroom delivery and practice the resources which enhance productivity. It is expected to deliver a novel means to the Knowledge

Education Framework via this whole exercise, which delivers, exploration, orientation and deliberations by the teachers who partner to the promotion of their schools.

A hypothesis framework for new age smart learning knowledge network:

Conclusion:

We relate to a common hub to provide a knowledge base to schools on cloud with easy access to the modules and the information. Here we need to provide a definite data security and satisfaction from the end of the clients to promote the learning community with co- ordination of Teachers/ Students/ Parents with Management in view of all towards productivity. The hubs designed and propagated regard to a spectrum of Knowledge delivery making each and every student of the school to be a collaborator to the knowledge canvas via the cloud. As we rightly believe in the fact that, for education delivery to function and happen, chalk and board is not enough for the teaching system. What is required is a **smile**, an opportunity to the students to **create**, **involve** and **explore** through ICT as the novel ways of understanding the subject further.

Teacher, the Educator should use technology to its fullest of wisdom and capacity available and the cloud format offers him the liberty to work beyond school hours 24x7 with ease of his comfort from home. The sole objective is to explore the magic of a cloud-based learning platform which is changing the way in which teachers and learners are embracing web technologies.

The implementation if explored as a complete knowledge hub would make the teaching/ learning process easy, interesting and result oriented. In the 21st century, a teacher must make efforts for digital learning as technology is not going to replace teachers, but those who don't use technology will be replaced by those do.

Features like uploading and downloading for the stake holders tend to expertise the learning density in a big way. It is far sound to govern with this capsule but a lot is required to generate from the end of the vendors to provide what is expected and granted initially as a Tailor Made solution and then ultimately being grounded onto a common fabric towards acceptance in mass.

References:

1. *ijcrt.com/UploadedArticle/16.pdfDHEERAJ MEHROTRA TACKLING THE GENERATION IN THE CLASSROOMS. Volume 1, Issue.3,March. 2013. International Journal Of*

Creative Research

2. *www.indianexpress.com/news/-today-internet- not-a...a...-/1026475/ Nov 4, 2012 - ... to students," expressed a parent. Tags: Next Education India Private Limited · DheerajMehrotra*

3. *longbeachparking.org/effective-teaching- methods.htm A good showcase by Dr DheerajMehrotra for all teachers to learn how to LEARN and then TEACH. Remember what we learnt once upon a time is no longer of .*

4. *independent.academia.edu/DheerajMehrotraSchool Management and Leadership, Education Politics and Planning, School-Public Relations and Adult Education. and ICT in Education, E-learning,Quality ...*

5. *edtechreview.in/news/.../364-tackling-tech-savvy-generation-in-classroo... This is a a guest post by Dr.DheerajMehrotra, Vice President (Academic Training/ School Audits) Next Education India Pvt Ltd. Walls and Friend Requests have ...*

Books By The Same Author

Available At Amazon!

Available At Amazon!

Available At Amazon!

Available At Amazon!

Available At Amazon!

Available at Amazon!

Available at Amazon!

Available at Amazon!

Available at Amazon!

Author Receiving the National Award by the President of India (Year 2006)

About The Author:

Dr. Dheeraj Mehrotra is an Educational Innovator, Author, with expertise in Six Sigma In Education, Academic Audits, Neuro Linguistic Programming (NLP), Total Quality Management In Education.

A former Principal at De Indian Public School, New Delhi, (INDIA), Dr. Dheeraj brings over two decades of teaching and training experience. He has authored over 70 books and is a certified Trainer for Quality Circles / TQM in Education and QCI Standards for School Accreditation and Six Sigma in Education. Dr. Dheeraj has trained over 6000 faculty and senior personnel in the education sector. His former workstations include, Boys' High School, Allahabad, Bishop Johnson School, Allahabad, City Montessori School, Lucknow, GEMS Education, Gurgaon, NEXT Education, Hyderabad.

Awards and Recognitions

President of India's National Teacher Award in the year 2006,

Best Science Teacher State Award (By the Ministry of Science and Technology, State of UP),

Education World – Best Teacher Award,

BOLT Learner Teacher Award by Air India,

'Innovation in Education Award 2016' by Higher Education Forum (HEF), Gujarat Chapter,

Developed over 150 FREE EDUCATIONAL MOBILE Apps for the Google Play Store exclusively for Teachers, Students and Parents. This work has been recognized by the LIMCA BOOK OF RECORDS & INDIA BOOK OF RECORDS. He is also a premium UDEMY Instructor with over 300 online published courses being circulated in over 180 plus countries.

www.authordheerajmehrotra.com
www.dheerajmehrotra.com